Nun Funnies!

cartoons by
Joe Lane

published by About Comics, Camarillo, California

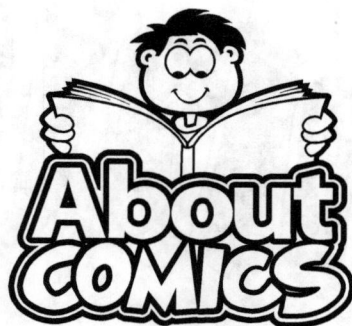

"I think I may say without fear of contradiction—"

"How many?"

"One!"

"Father, please do forgive us our trespasses!"

3

THE NUNMOBILE

"Thank God they're tucked in safely . . . I was worried sick
about them at the picnic!"

"Tow that wreck out of here!"

"Oh, no trouble, officer—we're just waiting 'till our hour is up."

"This car needs overhauling, Sister Bertha.
It keeps dragging in the rear."

"I don't know, Dominic. It just doesn't sound right!"

"Give us everything that's free!"

THE NUNMOBILE

"Oh, Father—you're the answer to our prayers!"

"Oh, well — thy will be done!"

"I think it needs oil."

"I'm taking it in for the 1,000 mile check-up."

"What discount can we get if you take out the cigarette lighter?"

"It's such a beautiful day, Sister—Let's put the top down."

THE NUNMOBILE

"Oh, dear—this happens every time I have to back up!"

"Not too fast now, Father, be careful—
Look out—Slow down—"

"We were so carried away by your magnificent metropolis,
officer, that we were unaware of whither we wentest!"

"*You shouldn't have passed him, Sister Bernard,
that's the Bishop!*"

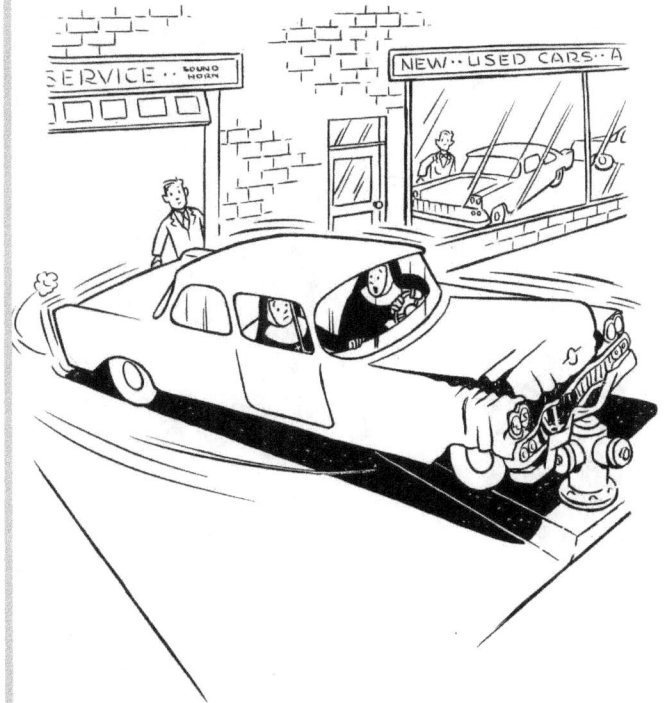

"*Well, Sister Matthias,
that takes care of the 'breaking in' period!*"

"*But, Sister Imelda Marie, we're not permitted to visit!*"

THE NUNMOBILE

"And may we assume that radio, heater, seat covers, power steering, power brakes and their ilk are included in your fabulous full price of $50?"

"Thank Heaven! Home at last!!"

"Say hello to Sister."

"You take this house, Sister Ervin. I'll go next door."

NATURE'S BEASTS

"Look, Sister Willene, one of God's little——

——creatures."

"Remember, Lucifer, love thy neighbor!"

"All I asked was—'Sister, will you bait the hook?'"

"Good conduct? Not you, Willie!"

"And here is one organization that throws very little business our way!"

"Going up . . . second floor . . . Sisters' reading room, dining palace, sewing salon, third floor, sleeping suites, solarium, going u-u-up!"

"Don't touch her, Mike . . . she's consecrated . . . use the shovel!"

"Does this look cleaner now?"

"Trick or treat!"

"Trick or treat!"

"Chartreuse thread, anyone?"

DOMESISTIC

CHRISTMAS LIST
~~MOM~~
~~DAD~~
~~MARY~~
~~SISTER~~
BROTHER

"This, I assume, is the automatic dryer."

"We need someone to play Santa, Sister, and we were wondering if . . ."

"And have you been a good little girl?"

DOMESISTIC

"Dig that design! Why, Mother, that's real cool!"

"Come on out, Sister, and get some suntan!"

"We'll start the day with the
morning offering . . ."

DOMESISTIC

"And who left this in the bathtub?"

"You gave me 3¢ too much change."

"Oh, it's lovely, Sister Mary Adelgond,
but give me the old coal and wood stove."

"Happy birthday to you . . ."

"Look, Sister . . . Captain Hook!"

"I don't care what he says about the low pressure area and the high pressure area, my corns forecast rain!"

'The latest poll shows 5 for Marian blue, 4 want angel white, 6 for papal yellow, 3 for cherub pink . . .'

"So long, neighbors!"

"To whom do we pray to get a refrigerator like that?"

". . . Er, is the lady of the house in?"

"Come in, Reverend Mother. We're having a bull session!"

"I don't know, Sister, but I thought the book was much better!"

"But, Sister Dorothea, everyone wears make-up on TV!"

"Now there, no doubt, Sister Grace, is something fraught with meaning!"

"Oh, Sister, you shouldn't have — I have everything!"

"Nothing, thanks . . . just looking."

"Is there also a Mickey Mouse cartoon?"

"Sandra Glamure—why, she used to be in my class
as Mathilda with the runny nose!"

"Come on, all you wranglers, the Chuck Wagon's ready!"

"Even with pay-TV, Sister Thomas More, we use our set just as much as before!"

"Sister will see you, Father, as soon as she's finished with Bishop Sheen."

"My word! She's quite a flapper!"

"Thank you, Sister. Now is there anyone else there with you?"

"Sister Carlotta also teaches geometry."

"Who wants apple pie?"

"Come into the kitchen and peel the apples."

"Hello . . . super-mart? Do you have any cereals with not quite so much pep and energy?"

"Look, Sister, crepes suzette!"

"These recipes are all very good, Sister, but my current date likes nothing but pizza pie!"

"Nice, juicy hash . . . smothered with leftovers."

"You may eat that taffy apple when the bell rings for lunch."

"Our sewing teacher."

"Please, St. Jude, do the impossible!"

"Methodius always said he'd have his own business some day."

"There are twenty-three of us and we must have our potatoes
all the same size."

"Er, could we have a peanut butter and jelly on rye?"

"Sister Fridian, I think the pilot light is out in this stove!"

"What will I do, Sister? This recipe calls for brandy!"

"$3.75 for just two of us . . . why, Sister, I can feed our whole convent for that!"

"Sister Mary Dorothea spent quite some time on the islands!"

"And may I say, Sister Mercita, in all my travels I've never seen a better job of camouflage on hash than yours!"

"We'll start off with a cocktail . . .

. . . Shrimp, that is!"

"For me, this is a light collation!"

"Father's just back from giving a mission in Texas."

"And here, Sister Adrian, is our walk-up apartment."

"The time? Oh, I guess it's about July or August, Sister."

MISSION HO!

"Well, anyway, Sister Grace,
it does have that lived-in look!"

"And this is our wash machine, Sister."

"Up here, Sister Henrica, we use the large missal
for our night prayers."

*"And this, Sister Benedicta,
we use in case of a heavy dew!"*

*"Of course, Sister Adrian, you'll find things a bit changed
when you get back to the States!"*

"Looks like real mission country, Sister Andre!"

"I'm spending my vacation down in the South American missions. How's about you?"

"Sister, this is Sister St. Pius, your summer replacement."

"Before you give us your spiel, may I say we have about $1.17 between the lot of us."

"No, thanks, Miss, we use holy water."

"Ah, good Sister, could you aid and abet one who has fulfilled his class prophecy of being the one least likely to succeed?"

47

"Anything you care to donate is deductible on your income tax."

"Twenty-four pairs of bobby sox?"

"Nothing, thanks . . . just looking."

"Do we pay for it in this world or can we wait 'til the next?"

"Remember now, the truth, the whole truth and nothing but, so help you!"

"Your policies sound wonderful, Mr. Williams, but the least of our worries are death benefits."

"We don't have quite enough in cash, but we could remember you in our novenas!"

"Send this to the grocer, the butcher and the coal man . . . 'I have your previous statements, and may I say we are making a novena to St. Joseph for funds?   As soon as he answers our prayers, you will receive a check. Sincerely . . .' "

"That'll be $18.74, Sister."

" . . . six hundred twenty-one, six hundred twenty-two, six hundred. . . ."

"I wish, Sister Patricia Anne,
we could AFFORD all the economy sizes!"

"We'll have to start another novena for funds,
Sister Mary Bilhild. Our creditors demand payment!"

"How about $50.00 cash
and the balance in trading stamps?"

NUN MONEY

"They're twenty-five cents a chance . . . five for a dollar!"

"I hear her folks are well off . . ."

"We've come to render to Caesar!"

"Do you have a steady job, Sister?"

"But, Sister, we're supposed to help little old ladies across the street!"

"Splendid, Vernon, splendid—next week we'll try it with the strings on!"

"Sister says I do things to a piano that no one else can do!"

"Do you have 'Three O'Clock in the Morning' and 'Feather
Your Nest?' "

"Before we go to Midnight Services, Reverend Mother, would
it be permissible to give one toot?"

"Listen, Sister, he's playing our song!"

"Sister!"

"Sister, can you play Chopsticks?"

"Jam session, anyone?"

"Sh-boom! Sh-BOOM! Da-da-da-da-da-da-da-da-da-da-da-da!"

"Uh 1, uh 2, uh 3 . . ."

"Cease and desist with the jazz Music for Tonight, and get going on the classical practicing for today!"

"Well, fiddle dee dee!"

"Yes, I have a question — may we have that box when you're finished?"

"Stand back! Give Sister room!"

"Canasta, anyone?"

NUNS AT PLAY

"Now relax, children, nothing to be afraid of."

"We'll save you from those rustlers, Sister!"

"The varmints went that-a-way!"

"Just what sort of game is this Gin Rummy?"

"And what did you do in civilian life, Kenny?"

"Stand in the corner and say three Hail Marys."

"I can't. I only know one."

"This way, but please keep silence. . . . The Sisters are at prayer."

"I wonder if she's going to tell Father she took my water pistol!"

"After taking your medicine, Doctor, and making a novena to
St. Peregrine, I feel wonderful!"

"And no whispering or talking during classes, please!"

"No wonder Sister knows so much about men—she's got eight brothers!"

"Come quick, Sister, I think I've invented water!"

TEACHING SISTERS

"Quotation marks—today—comma—Father—comma Sister taught us
punctuation—period—quotation marks."

". . . And please help our team beat the daylights out of room six,
amen."

"And then there are times when I'd like to bash their little heads in!"

"I know God made me to know Him, to love Him, to serve Him in this world and be happy with Him forever in the next—but why did He make him?"

"Here, Sisters, is a specimen—

"—of live salamander!"

"A 40 in arithmetic, Kretlow, hardly makes me envision a tycoon in industry."

"Now I know why Father Clancy dismisses class with 'God be with you.'"

"So, Lefty, our trails cross again."

"Thanks for the extra study period, Mother—you're the most!"

"And now I see that my time is up—"

"Aloysius, why do you persist in being tardy?"

"Well, well, if it isn't my old WAC sergeant!"

"Something wrong, Sister? You look pale."

"Sister Ignatia used to work for Colossal Studios in Hollywood."

"This is the new pupil, Father—he's rather shy."

"My third graders do much better."

"Touché!"

"Sister's taking me to match wits with the Principal."

"When can we have another party, Sister?"

"Not enough room on the blackboard, Sister."

"Now let me tell you the cute things he does in class!"

"Sister'll be all right—had her first class today!"

① "John." "Here!" ② "Mary." "Present!"

③ "Joseph." "Here!" ④ "Peter." "Pray for us!"

EXAMINATION QUESTION

① 15 ÷ 3 =
② 25 ÷ 5 =
③ 30 ÷ 6 =
④ 27 ÷ 9 =

2 × 5 =
6 × 6 =
7 × 8 =
9 × 2 =
5 × 4 =

"Security regulations forbid me to divulge any information."

KINDERGARTEN CLASS of 195

"And now we leave these hallowed halls of learning to face the grim realities of the outside world."

"Sister Adora, is this one of the many ills the flesh is heir to?"

"Promoted to third grade - - - my, my,
you've come a long way, Turibius!"

"Please, Cub Scouts, not in uniform!"

"Pass out these papers, Milton, and let neither snow nor rain nor heat nor gloom of night stay you from the swift completion of your appointed rounds."

"Sister Willene is very impartial. No one gets a hundred!"

"I know, Sister Sulpice, I'm late — l-a-t."

"Who—er—whom shall I say is calling, Sister?"

"Almost broke my perfect attendance record today, Sister!"

"Peter and Thomas, stop that talking!"

'Do you really think she's got eyes in the back of her head?'

"Your logic is profoundly conclusive, Camillus—"

"And you justify your point of view very convincingly—"

"But you still must do homework!"

"Sister Thomas More, may we choose our category?"

"Under the spreading chestnut tree,
the village smithy stands, engaged
in a rather out-moded form of employment."

"It says I'll be a great success and have lots of children!"

"Hut—2—3—4—!"

"And if I had my life to live over again, Sister, I'd still wanna be in your room."

"Just a second there!"

"Just the facts, Kunnegunda—Just give me the facts!"

"Who stole the ding dong? Who stole the bell?"

"No help from the audience, please!"

"Dum de dum dum!"

"And now, a brief message from our sponsor."

TEACHING SISTERS

"Sister Mary Ignatia has one of the toughest classes in school!"

"Reverend Father, Venerable Sister, distinguished guests, members of my class . . . I don't know the answer!"

"But, Sister, he's only going through a phase!"

"This is a good time to ask the pastor for a new blackboard."

"Today I'm introducing my class to the use of pens."

"Halo, everybody, halo . . ."

"Sister, do you have ears?"

"I have to keep reminding myself they're children of God and heirs of Heaven!"

"And if he's naughty, Sister Humilissa, you have our permission to spank him!"

"*Are you majoring in Botany, Greeley?*"

"*To make a long story short, Sister Ivana, nyet!*"

"*Here's my note for being absent, Sister Mary Sulpice!*"

TEACHING SISTERS

"Sometimes, Miss Daly, it helps if you imagine
this as a part of your purgatory!"

"Yes, I certainly do have that dull, tired, dragged-out
feeling — You would, too, if you had my class!"

"Sorry Im late, Sister Agnesine, but I couldn't get more than 19,000 miles per hour out of my rocket ship!"

"Care to join me in a Novena to get transferred back into the jungles?"

"It's her first day in high school, Sister Ellarose. She's a little shy!"

93

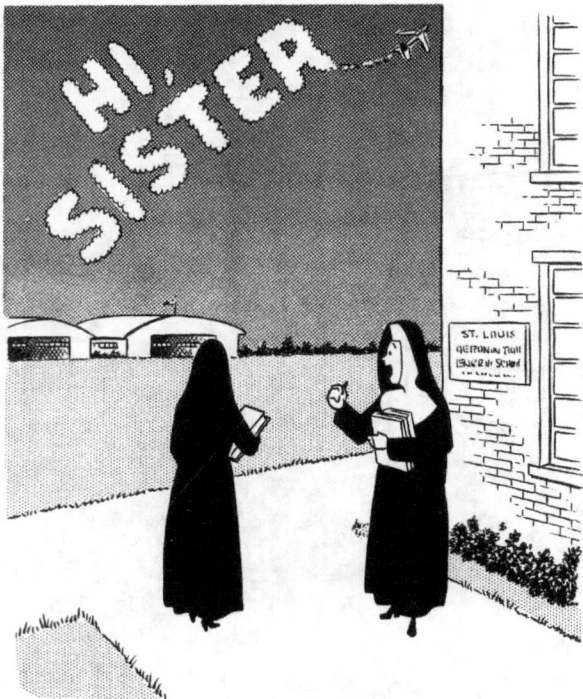

"That's Willie, Sister—
He always used to scribble on the blackboard!"

"Well, Doolittle, what's the excuse this time?"

"The class is very proud of Morrison, Sister Patrick,
he made his first 70 today."

94

"Oscar likes onion sandwiches."

"Before we begin, class, may I say this will be a
do-it-yourself test, and I DO mean, do it yourself!"

"Outer space is nothing new to Thaddeus—he's been
staring into it for the past semester and a half!"

"Well, outside of his school work,
Eddie is one of my smartest pupils!"

"At home, Sister Louisine, we simply ignore him!"

"One thing you'll find out—they're all born with concupiscence."

"I'll be glad to help you with your problem . . ."

"Sister's real proud of me, Mom. She says I'm quite an ordeal!"

TEACHING SISTERS

"... 'Take it easy, avoid excitement,' " he says. "I'd like to see him with a room full of sixth graders!"

"Sister knows so much about Lincoln, he must have been in her class!"

"If you guys ever need a lie detector . . ."

"Well, Adams, so far so good."

"Oh, oh! Muzynski's gone back to watching the late, late, late show!"

"Get thee behind me!"

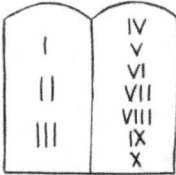

"Gee whiz, Sister! After we learn these, life ain't gonna be the same!"

"You have eight wrong, Thaddeus. Would you care to try for sixteen?"

"I just can't seem to get his confidence!"

"Is Itty Bitty Buddy Boy striving for a zero?"

"The poor marks, Antonson. Pourquois?"

"According to this, I didn't even reach the first plateau!"

"You're doin' a bang-up job wit' Lawrence, Sister Mary.
Ev'ry night he reads me the funnies!"

"Mrs. Kerr, why aren't you a nun?"

"From our Do-It-Yourself Club, Sister Allen. A token of our esteem!"

"How do you do, Sister? You doubtlessly have been spending a great deal of time wondering about the qualifications of our party candidates . . ."

"We just want you to know we're happy with all our presents!"

"We were sort of toying with the idea of Black!"

"Most unusual . . . want shoes that fit!"

"Please, Miss, where can we find the exit?"

"Let's just try this for size."

"Well, if it isn't Maggie O'Rourke! What've you been doing all these years?"

"A dozen pipe cleaners, please."

"Isn't it terrible, Sister? You can't get a thing for five dollars any more."

SHOPPING

"Hmph!"

"Some nice furniture . . . for the convent, perhaps?"

"Would you save us your cancelled stamps?"

"Sister Mercita, I wouldn't be caught dead in it!"

"*Could you suggest something for a Mother General?*"

"Quick, Sister, your beads—Notre Dame is losing!"

"It's easy, girls . . . see, just like one—two—three—O'Leary . . ."

"Can I borrow the catcher's mask, Sister?"

"Hurry, Willie, we're losing 12 to 0."

"Give me five minutes in that backfield and I'd put that game on ice."

"Sisters, the latest book on metaphysics is being reviewed at this time
on the educational channel!"

"The pastor would like to borrow his clubs this afternoon."

"And this is the big sizzler from the gridiron!"

"Could we watch the Notre Dame game while we make up our mind?"

"And unless you come up with a win today, I'll be back teaching kindergarten!"

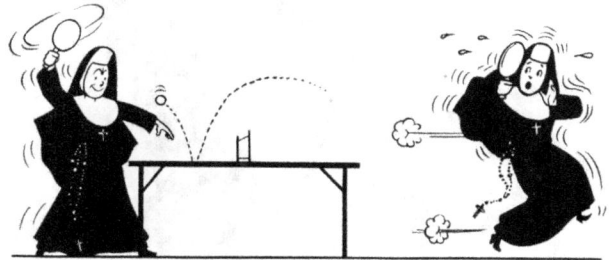

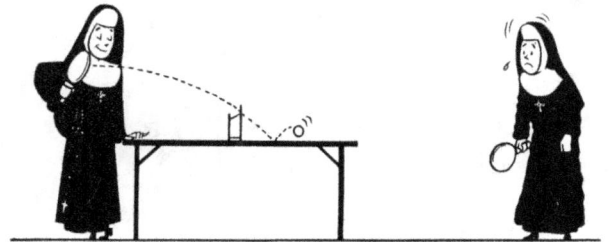

"No more fumbling . . . or, one of these days, Hennessy . . .
ONE OF THESE DAYS!"

"All right, now, you men try and stop me!"

"Who turned off the Notre Dame game?"

"Baseball, anyone?"

SPORTIN' NUNS

"I won't be out today, guys . . ."

"I have a previous commitment."

"I like home to be neat and tidy."

"Take me to your leader!"

"Imagine— two years ago she was known as 'Tuffy, the Roller Derby Terror'!"

"She spent five years in the WACS before coming here!"

"Believe me, if I had my life to live over again, I'd be a nun!"

"Eight nuns and one novice . . . put down eight and a half, Al."

"Mom and Dad, I'd like you to meet Mother Superior."

"Sorry, Mr. Greely, but I won't be at the supermart this summer!"

"The postulant's winter raiment in the novitiate differs somewhat from that of the outside world, Sister!"

"Sister will show you to your cells!"

"Cells???"

"And when do we get to mold little minds and build strong characters to face the vicissitudes of life?"

"We usually say, 'An error has been made', not, 'Somebody goofed'!"

"Now that, Sister Cordella,
is what I call encouraging a vocation!"

THROUGH THESE
PORTALS PASS THE
MOST BEAUTIFUL
GIRLS IN THE WORLD

"It's an expression that was quite popular in my day."

POSTULANTS'
DORMITORY

"Ludmilla, here in the Novitiate we strive to treat our postulants with deference, tenderness and understanding . . . and, if an occasion warrants . . . to mete out justice with kindness and clarity . . .

. . . So . . . what's the beef?"

"Look, Mom and Dad, my winter, spring, summer and fall outfit!"

"Since we got our TV set, we rarely use our record player."

"I don't want to be a brilliant woman, Sister. I want to be a nun, like you!

"He was very much interested in my kindergarten class."

"Now watch — they'll ask for some island no one has ever heard of!"

"The diner's open."

"You be my beneficiary, Sister, and I'll be yours!"

"Sister, are you from Mars?"

"Don't forget, Sister, drop in any time."

"Oh, we stick pretty close to home!"

THE TRAVELIN' NUNS

"Take us out on the road to St. Margaret's Convent, and when the meter reads thirty-five cents, we'll get out and walk the rest."

"Oh, it isn't too bad—but the roofs leak."

"Now to find the motherhouse!"

"I must say, Sister, I have better deportment in my classroom!"

"Do you suppose it would be all right,
Sister Madeline Marie? I hear it's made by monks!"

"It must be a treat for you Sisters to get outside the convent walls once in a while!"

"This looks like my room after one of our kindergarten parties!"

"Young man, are you in the state of grace?"

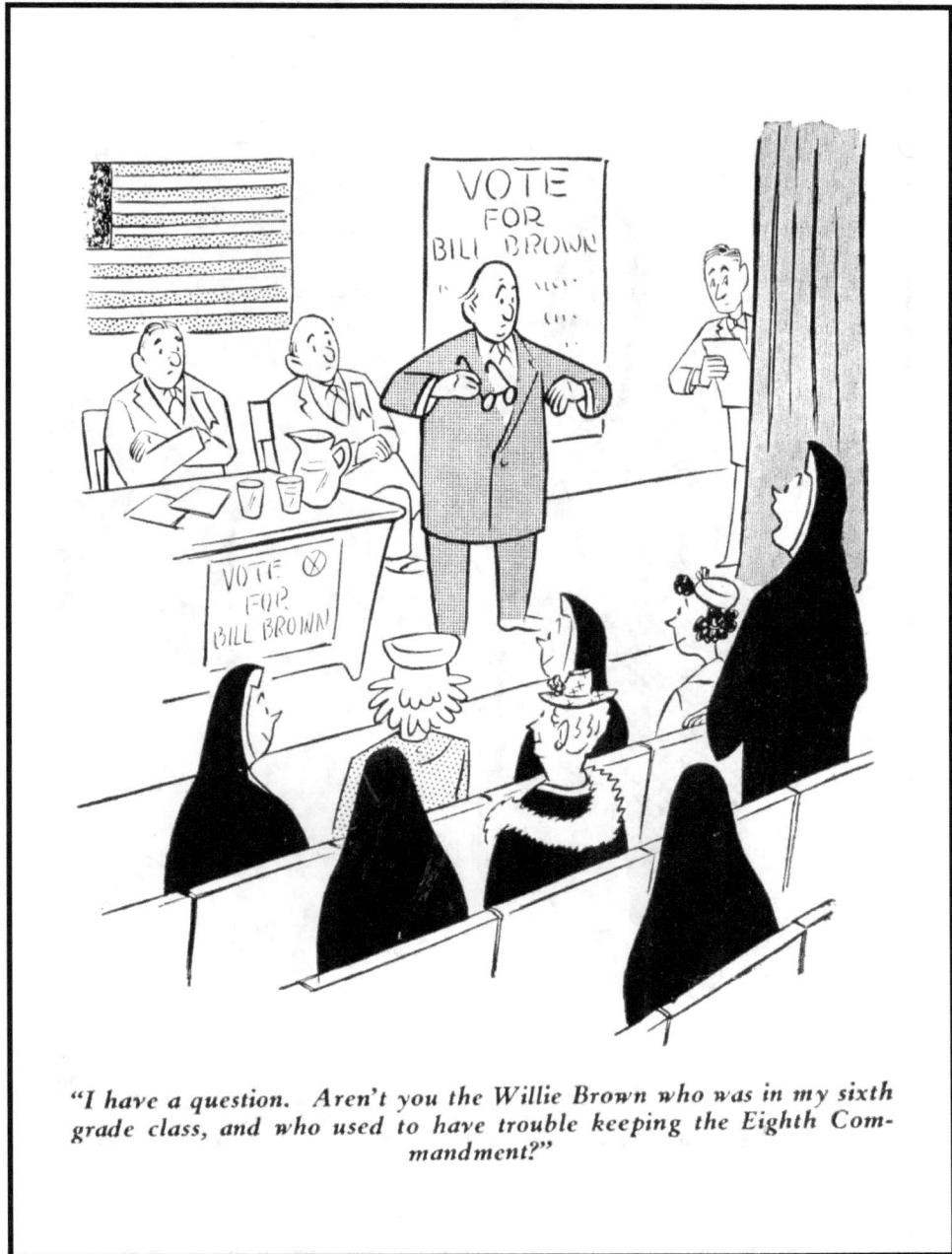

"I have a question. Aren't you the Willie Brown who was in my sixth grade class, and who used to have trouble keeping the Eighth Commandment?"

"*We need honest watchers at the polls. . . . Should we ask them?*"